INSIGHT 101

INSIGHT 101

The Way of Big Power

Randy B. Haskins

author*HOUSE*®

AuthorHouse™
1663 Liberty Drive
Bloomington, IN 47403
www.authorhouse.com
Phone: 1-800-839-8640

Published by AuthorHouse   07/13/2012

ISBN: 978-1-4772-3290-3 (sc)
ISBN: 978-1-4772-3289-7 (e)

Library of Congress Control Number: 2012911834

Any people depicted in stock imagery provided by Thinkstock are models, and such images are being used for illustrative purposes only.
Certain stock imagery © Thinkstock.

This book is printed on acid-free paper.

I dedicate this book to my four instructors, William M. Whitley Sensei, Takeshi Okamura Sensei, Noriyasu Kudo Sensei and Life. To my mother, brothers and grandmother. Thank you for directing me to the path of enlightenment and presenting me with the tools needed in order to begin my journey. I would also like to thank my daughter for her birth and for causing my re-birth.

Est. 1996

Written by: Randy B. Haskins
Edited by: Iris Broudy, Leila H. Haskins & Randy B. Haskins
Cover design by: Randy B. Haskins
All photo's courtesy of: Underground Alliance archives

Contents

Introduction

I have a vision. My vision is of a martial art that does what all arts were intended to do; work for everyone, against anyone, at any given time. How can this happen? By approaching all technique with common sense and a natural flow. This piece of literature is a gateway into the mind of one who has been a student of the fighting arts for more than three decades. I have had the honor of studying classical arts as well as modern arts. I have come to realize a few things as a result of my research. The essays that I have written will act as a window into the soul of martial arts as it is taught today. It's been said that, "Admitting that there is a problem is the first step on the road to recovery." Here is the first step, lets take it together. OSU!

Randy B. Haskins
(Hachidan)

1

SO, YOU HAVE A BLACK BELT? WHO CARES!

Fifty years ago people were in awe of those who achieved the rank of black belt. Those who were dedicated enough to do so were considered the elite, and for good reason. Back then nothing was given away, everything was earned. In that time the now infamous black belt meant something, but now everyone has one. Many things have contributed to the lack of quality Dan (Black Belt) holders in this day and age. Lack of knowledgeable instructors, business-oriented instructors and unmotivated students, just to name a few. Due to the abundant quantity of unqualified black belts, we are looked down upon. So how do we bring back the views of the past? The answer is simple. We must utilize the mirror in the dojo and look to *develop the self*.

DEVELOP THE SELF

Inside any dojo you can find mirrors covering almost every wall. As you train you are taught to gaze into those mirrors so that you may develop the proper form to your technique. There is also a deeper purpose for this gaze. You are encouraged to look at the self. As you train, develop and strengthen every aspect of the self, (motivated with pure intentions) you will become the best person, martial artist and human being that you could possibly be. If each practitioner *took the time to understand* what each rank that he/she wore truly meant, society as a whole would place black belts back on that pedestal.

TAKE THE TIME TO UNDERSTAND

Due to the fact that styles have varying ranking structures, I will not discuss specific belts. I will discuss three stages of the training process. The stages are beginner, intermediate and advanced.

BEGINNER LEVEL

At this level a person is innocent, unknowing, almost child-like. The focus of one's training at this point is geared towards etiquette. The practitioner is taught how to conduct him/herself in the presence of fellow practitioners, senior students, black belts and instructors. One also learns how to conduct oneself before, during and after a training session. The lessons learned extend far beyond the dojo. They are very much a part of everyday life. Respect, common courtesy and honor are the foundation of a warrior lifestyle.

INTERMEDIATE LEVEL

At this level, while proper etiquette is still observed, a practitioner is encouraged to concentrate on executing techniques with proper form. Anyone at this stage of their training must also model proper etiquette for the beginners in and out of the dojo. Although, repetition is stressed all through one's training, it is strongly concentrated on at this level. Following suit with the child-like mentality at the beginner level, a student at this level is regarded as having a teenage mentality.

ADVANCED LEVEL

Advanced-level students are responsible for much of the dojo's operation. Advanced students must ensure that the instructor is not burdened with trivial issues such as finances, questions from beginners, chore delegation and challenge matches. Students responsibilities at the advanced level are endless, in and out of the dojo. A student at this level is now considered a serious beginner, and is encouraged to re-evaluate his/her techniques. Re-evaluating ones techniques is a process that will happen countless times within the training process.

CONCLUSION

This article is a brief overview of practitioners responsibilities at three stages of their development. With a strong desire to learn, and a will to work hard, one realizes that the journey never ends. I believe in the ***ELITE BLACK BELT!*** How about you?

2

THE TRUE ESSENCE OF KATA

The first thing I want you to do is grab a brand new pencil, # 2 if you've got it. OK, now hold it between your pointer finger and thumb on each hand, apply downward pressure with your two pointer fingers and upward pressure with your thumbs. What happened?

Now I would like you to take your obi, a towel, a shoe lace or anything else constructed in the same manner. Grab it in both hands and proceed to apply pressure. Can you break it?

What does that little experiment tell you? Think relaxed, free flowing, non-restricted power. Rigidity breaks down when enough pressure is applied. Flexibility has unlimited potential. Be flexible in mind as well as body.

I graduated from a trade school in Springfield, Massachusetts with a heating and air conditioning concentration. The first thing shown to our class was the tools that we would be using throughout our careers in our field. Martial arts are no different. The first aspect of training is one being taught basic techniques. I.e. straight punch, reverse punch, front kick, etc . . . . you get my point, *our tools*.

The second aspect of training begins after one is proficient in the physical execution of all techniques (tools) within the particular style that one studies. This aspect consists of one being introduced to a **concept** and the **theory** that supports it. The practitioner is then introduced to a combination consisting of two or more of the techniques learned in the first aspect. The combination introduced is only an example of how to achieve that particular concept.

Just in case you were wondering exactly what the difference between a concept and a theory is. In a nutshell, a concept is what one plans to do and the theory would be why one plans to do it. For example, a concept would be *blind spot positioning.* The theory is, once that position is achieved, uke's retaliatory, defensive, and offensive options are greatly limited, while tori's offensive options are maximized.

Now we are at the point in our training where we begin to learn the kata that our respective styles have to offer. There are a couple of points that have to be made concerning kata. First, we must understand the title of the kata itself in order to begin to understand its purpose. Each kata was designed with a purpose in mind, i.e. self-defense focused or exercises focused. We must also recognize the importance of practicing kata and not performing kata. If we practice kata, we will have an opportunity to unlock the hidden aspects of the kata in question. Lastly, we must explore the four phases of learning kata: **bunkai**, **oyo**, **henka** and **kakushi**.

The first phase is bunkai. Bunkai speaks on the visual perception/analysis of the techniques/combinations. The technique that I will use to help me make my point is an upward block. Would you be able to perceive when an upward block is being used within a kata? More than likely "yes" would be the answer given 100% of the time. That is what I mean by visual perception. In essence that phase is dedicated to learning the patterns and movements of the kata as taught by one's instructor.

I remember **Noriyasu Kudo Sensei** saying to me, "The problem with most people and their lack of ability to effectively defend themselves, is that they try to execute techniques in the street exactly the way they perform them in their kata." Which leads us to the next phase of practicing kata.

In this phase we evaluate our kata using the principles of oyo. Oyo is the process of adjusting a particular technique to make it more realistic for the street. Imagine, uke (receiver of technique) grabbing tori's (deliverer of technique) lapel with his/her right hand. Harmonizing with uke's movement, tori executes an upward block as uke's arm fully extends during the reaching process. Here's the adjustment. Tori's retracting hand (left) grabs uke's wrist in a hooking fashion while his extending arm (right) smashes against uke's elbow, causing it to hyper extend and break. The principle of ***sen no sen*** (early initiative) was employed in this scenario.

Kakushi brings us back in history to when the Chinese masters had disguised their intentions by giving techniques names like "*Buddha sitting on a lotus.*" Kakushi, simply put, is the hidden purpose. Visual perception leads one to believe that the movement in the execution of an upward block is just that, an upward block. In actuality in the scenario presented, what appeared to be a block was in fact an arm break. As you see, applying the principles of oyo leads you to discover kakushi.

Henka is the next phase of learning a kata. Exploring kata through the principles of henka helps one to achieve the ability to adjust to ever-changing conditions, circumstances and situations. Imagine the same scenario as mentioned in the last paragraph, only this time tori misses the window of opportunity to hyper extend uke's arm due to poor timing. Tori now must adapt using the principles of O.O.D.A, (**o**bserve, **o**rient, **d**ecide, **a**ct). Uke successfully grabs tori and pulls him/her close, so tori now executes a combination wrist flex, knife hand strike to uke's neck. The principle of *late initiative (Go no Sen)* had to be employed because of timing.

As an intelligent individual I recognize the truth that punching and kicking could not have been the only form of fighting back in the days when the masters designed their kata. Why wouldn't kata address other forms of combat such as grabbing, seizing, throwing, as well as striking arts?

There was a time when an instructor would enter a dojo and begin to work out, as if he were alone. All those who were allowed to follow had to do just that, follow. No words were spoken. Everyone in the dojo imitated the master's movements. When the master felt that a particular student was the one worth grooming to be his/her successor the master would explore all other aspects of practicing the kata of his particular style with him/her. All others were left with their visual perception of the techniques.

All martial principles interconnect one way or another. With proper practice of kata coupled with serious investigation of the history of the kata anyone can unlock the mysteries surrounding true combat. I've honestly rarely ever met anyone who had true working knowledge of kata and its benefits, yet many claim to be masters. Interesting!

No wonder so many people such as Bruce Lee and all those "reality fighters" speak so badly about classical arts and their kata. The so-called "masters" and their lack of knowledge, as well as their inability to successfully utilize the lessons learned in the dojo while on the streets, keep people laughing at us. The traditional/classical martial artists.

Noriyasu Kudo Kancho & Tommy Rondeau Shihan

3

DID YOU KNOW? APPARENTLY NOT!

When I began my search for an instructor to teach me what Bruce Lee made look so easy, I did not like the things that instructors were saying to me. It seemed like everyone who claimed to be a sensei wanted my money but had no idea what theories would best fit my body or personality. I eventually found someone who understood the essence of being an instructor, and quickly joined his dojo. I've been a member in good standing ever since. I achieved my shodan rank (1st degree black belt) on March 2, 1991. Since then I've visited several other dojos and spoke to many instructors. Thinking back to those conversations, I find one thing evident: The ***American martial artist has no idea what the difference is between a fighter and a warrior***.

Fighting is an instinctual act that anyone will engage in when he/she feels threatened. Individuals have different tolerance levels for different issues, and some individuals act out physically when they hit that so-called "wall". There are also fighting sports where there is no honor involved. Usually those sport shows are all about entertainment and money. I've witnessed several of those fight-oriented sport shows where the combatants displayed poor sportsmanship. How many times have you gone out to a bar or sat outside on a hot summer day and witnessed two or more individuals engaged in a physical altercation over trivial issues? I can go on and on with example after example, but I won't. I'm sure you get the point. ***ANY FOOL CAN FIGHT!***

Warriors live by an unwritten moral code called **BUSHIDO**. Those who train in the martial arts use the mirror as a source of enlightenment. The seven precepts of **BUSHIDO** that guide a warrior's existence are: <u>Benevolence</u>, <u>Veracity</u>, <u>Courage</u>, <u>Honor</u>, <u>Loyalty</u>, <u>Politeness</u>, and <u>Justice</u>. Many people claim to be warriors, but very few truly understand what it is to be one. Warriors don't claim to be anything, they simply are. I must clear up a misconception. A warrior doesn't necessarily have to be a martial artist. In a nutshell, ***a warrior is someone who understands what it is to care and cares enough to understand***.

Demonstrating a front kick for my daughter (Randi) 4th kyu

4

GOALS

Training is a life-long endeavor that produces very tangible results. There are many benefits that one will gain as a result of proper dedicated practice. I will discuss the benefits received in a simplified form. I break it down into three parts: **Body**, **mind**, and **spirit**.

The **body** represents the techniques or the physical aspect of training. This part is a never-ending process. Through proper dedicated practice one could achieve a technically proficient front kick but then receive injuries from an automobile accident. Now one has to modify or retrain oneself as a result of one's newfound limitation. Many factors can contribute to modification, such as age, injury and personality.

The **mind** represents the common-sense theories as applied to combat. Once the mental capacity is achieved, it is rarely lost. In this area, one has to commit the concepts and theories to more than just memory. Through proper dedicated practice one begins to truly understand and believe the concepts and theories.

When we discuss **spirit** we are referring to an individual's "will" and ultimately an individual's state of enlightenment. In short, through attaining the skill to fight, one begins to understand the theory of *universal harmony*. And as a result, understands when and when-not to fight, how to fight, and where to fight.

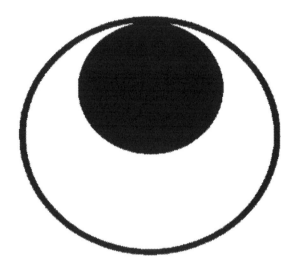

In & Yo

Randi practicing her front kick

5

NEVER IMPOSE

One of Bruce Lee's most famous statements is, "Be like water my friend, be like water." Several masters of the martial arts express that very same sentiment, and for good reason. Water is one of nature's most formidable elements. It destroys things with gradual ease as well with quick destructive power. Water also has life-sustaining capabilities. Considering water's attributes, many could not argue against Lee's idea. I, on the other hand, subscribe to a different school of thought.

I aspire to emulate wind. Think about it. What can you actually do to the wind and what can the wind do to you? Bruce was right when he said, "If you put water in a cup, it becomes the cup. Put it in a jar, it becomes the jar." But, it is also *trapped* in the jar. Wind is a powerful element that can blow roofs off of houses, destroy bridges, trees and buildings. Whatever it can't uproot, it damages by creating cross winds.

Wind is odorless, but can carry odors. It is also silent, unless an object obstructs it. It can't be trapped, just generated. Wind can be pleasant or dangerous. Nature itself is the strongest force known to man. So why fight it? **Never impose your will on nature, let nature lead the way.**

Me teaching a seminar in Chicopee, Ma., student pictured above is Rolando Pagan

6

A DOSE OF REALITY

This letter was written in response to **The Winning Edge** article that appeared in the January 2000 issue of the **Black Belt Magazine**. The article discussed the idea of the government stepping in regulating all martial arts promotions and instructor certifications.

The letter reads:

I agree with the regulation of the martial arts instructor certification wholeheartedly. I believe that each individual organization should step up and regulate their own. The problem lies within the American martial arts community's lack of knowledge of, or total disregard for, the true history behind the ranks and titles that we wear.

First of all, the 1st degree black belt means that the wearer is nothing more than a serious beginner. A person is not eligible to even apply for a teaching certificate until he/she is a 3rd degree black belt. A black belt certificate and a license to teach are two very different certificates. Not everyone will qualify as an instructor. Some will never earn the right to teach because they have no teaching ability.

As a black belt of any degree you will always be considered a Sempai (Advanced Practitioner). As a 3rd degree black belt you are now eligible to become a Sensei (Teacher). As a 5th degree you're eligible to become a Shihan (Master Teacher). As a 9th degree you're eligible to hold the title of Professor.

There are many other titles used within the martial arts community. The four listed above are among the most common. The titles do not come as you achieve the ranks corresponding with the title. They are separate unto themselves. All those who claim to be true martial artists need to investigate the history behind ranks and titles. Titles should not be used as loosely as they are.

Individual martial arts organizations need to promote accordingly and assign ranks/titles the way they are designed to be used. If the individual organizations won't pick up the slack and regulate correctly, then I'm all for someone stepping in and taking control.

Me (Hachidan)

7

WHAT IS IT WITH THE KARATE YELL?

There are many different views on the subject, "The karate yell, spirit shout, internal energy generated by the focused." I remember sitting in a dojo with **Takeshi Okamura Sensei** (Daito Ryu Aiki Jujutsu) observing a karate class. The young students were being instructed in the execution of the kata of their system. They were yelling the word "kiai" as they executed strikes. Sensei leaned over to me and asked, "Why are they yelling that word?" I just shrugged my shoulders and smiled. The truth is, I was wondering the exact same thing.

Ki energy can be felt and expressed a few different ways. First, let me share with you my view of what ki energy actually is. Ki is energized action without doubt. What do I mean? Well, most people believe that they can't lift a car, but once a loved one is trapped underneath it, without thinking or hesitation they react and lift it. Martial artists train to be able to command that type of energy at will.

Years ago I was told the following story. Long ago in 16th century Japan, a samurai's family had been killed by a tiger. Distraught about that fact, the samurai embarked on a mission to kill the tiger. As the samurai was searching the jungle, he spotted the tiger or what appeared to be the tiger at least fifty paces away. He drew a bolt (arrow), raised his bow and released. The arrow was right on target. He hit center mass. The arrow went straight through the tiger. The samurai advanced to check his prey for any signs of life. When he reached the tiger, he realized that what he had in fact shot was not the tiger. It was a boulder. Amazed, he stepped back about fifty paces and attempted the very same feat, to no avail. This time, the arrow hit the boulder and broke. Why?

The samurai had been totally focused on the task at hand. All of his training had come into play at that moment. His mind was devoid of all doubt. He merely reacted. Everything was in line. His breathing, focus, energy transfer, form, balance, skill, and his ability to harmonize with the universe were one.

The kiai or spirit shout is a verbalization of one's state of focus. When you are lifting weights or pushing a car, you dig down deep and grunt. Why? I'll tell you why. An energy release. Some people might say that ki is no more than an adrenalin dump. I'm here to tell you that it is much deeper than that. Anyone who truly practices an art will agree.

How you exhale during a strike or activation of a pressure point will affect the desired result. Not many have access to knowledgeable instructors to really explore this aspect of training, but trust me, they are out there.

I had an experience that most would not believe. One day, not too long ago. I was training with a couple of friends. Mark Whitley Sensei was leading us. Sensei was leading the class in kata and we were all following along when I felt what I would call a major energy surge. I stopped executing my kata, looked around. and seen that I wasn't the only one who felt this. We all just stood there looking dumbfounded, staring at Whitley Sensei.

He was totally oblivious to what was happening. To the fact that we all had stopped and were now watching him. After he ended his kata, he wanted to work on some throws and their counters. We all grabbed partners, I was his. As I attempted to throw Sensei, he countered by neutralizing my hip. His shin slightly touched my leg. OK, here's where it gets crazy.

My leg was now on fire. As I lifted my gi pant leg, I was shocked to see what appeared to be a burn spanning across the space that Sensei's leg had just touched. All the others in the room were inquiring what had happened to me because they saw the burn as well. I know it sounds kind of outlandish, but I'm here to tell you it is entirely true.

Silent ki, as well as energy transfers are very real elements to be explored by students of the martial arts. I encourage all who are truly interested to seek real instruction from a **qualified** teacher.

8

TRANSMISSION

Imagine this. Tell me if this is a possible scenario. A great master is sought out by many who would like to train in his particular style of martial arts. He is very selective. He does not run a commercial dojo. He is very much a traditionalist. He is not consumed with worldly possessions, or fortune and fame. He is very humble by nature, and very much dedicated to the true essence of his martial art. If he were living now, he would not be impressed or even interested in a magazine like *Black Belt*. He is a dedicated student, effective fighter, knowledgeable instructor and the world's greatest advocate for peace and harmony.

As time passes he accepts a small following of students, seven to be exact. Sensei enters the dojo, located in a small room in the back of his house every morning at 5am, bows in, and proceeds to work out as if he were alone. The students are given three rules to follow. (1.) Always be on time, (2.) Follow his lead, and (3.) Never question anything. They all do as they are told. As time progresses, two students are excused from the dojo and two more are accepted. The advanced practitioners are easily distinguished by having dirtier sashes than the newer students.

At this time colored belts haven't been invented yet, so everyone is wearing a white sash to hold his/her jacket closed. Skill and knowledge are the determining factors as to who is or isn't a master. The only way to distinguish between who is or isn't a master is by engaging in challenge matches fought to the death. Those who established themselves were considered the elite, and for good reason.

(In this day and age, the here and now, everyone is a "grand master" and most haven't a clue as to what it actually means to be one. Many also haven't even met, much less had, an opportunity to train under a qualified instructor. The state of martial arts is a joke!)

Thirty years into training the master selects one of his students to be his successor. Up until this point, training has consisted of the students imitating the master's movements during kata practice, with no verbal exchange whatsoever. The student selected is instructed to attend more training sessions, which are set at odd times in the early morning hours. He is also allowed to sit and have tea with the master. During those extra sessions the master passes on the history of his art. The student is also allowed to ask questions. During those early morning sessions the student is introduced to the deeper phases of kata practice. The other six students are left with only their visual perception of what they have imitated all these years.

A few more years pass. The master falls ill, and is on his death bed. The master presents his disciple with the Menkyo Kaiden (certificate of full proficiency) in his art. He is now the second generation head master of that ryu. The new head master refuses to break tradition and accepts a small group of students. One becomes his disciple, and is passed on the responsibility of transmitting the true essence of that art. Meanwhile, the other six break off after the death of the master and open their own schools, teaching what they have learned. Each school has an enrollment of 300 students. That's 1,800 students receiving incomplete information. 1,800 students receive black belts. Each trains 300 people to black belt. That's 540,000 new black belts with incomplete information. You get my point.

We have seen that in a lifetime of study a master will select one to whom he will pass on the in-depth information. All others are what we see in the limelight today. The masters are humble, unassuming, productive members of society harmonizing with the universe. So, is it possible!?

9

WHAT STYLE IS THE BEST?

How many times have you heard, "Who would win in a fight, Jackie Chan or Bruce Lee?" If I had a nickel for every time that someone asked me a question along that line I would be able to buy my own planet. How about the old favorite, "What style is the best?" People actually believe that styles have everything to do with a fighter's success in a street altercation. Styles are only foundations for one to build on. They are not the end-all, cure all. The problem is, as Bruce Lee has so eloquently stated several times in his life, "Individuals become bound by style."

Skill is not determined by the physical. It is determined by what one comes to realize about the physical. I know individuals who have trained for years and can execute techniques proficiently but don't know **how**, or **when**, to apply them in street encounters.

Lets take a look at the art of boxing. Boxing is a very effective form of fighting. Boxers are trained to take hits, deliver hits, and avoid hits. In the prison I work at, I've seen professional boxers defend themselves against multiple attackers with ease. On the other hand, I've seen boxers get destroyed with ease by individuals without comparable skill. That point proves that effectiveness in any style is an individual thing, and not a style thing.

If you take a look back at Iron Mike Tyson's career, or that of any other boxer who lost once and tried to come back, unsuccessfully, you will see what I mean. Iron Mike was fierce in the ring, as well as on the street. Just ask Mitch Green. Then, he lost to Buster Douglas. That pretty much was the end of his career. Terrible Terry Norris fell off the face of the earth after his first loss. Roy Jones Jr. tried to come back, to no avail. Then we have Mohammed Ali. A man who had the skill, heart, drive and fire to come back over and over again, and win, after losing.

Martial artists, who truly explore their art, will have the tools necessary to effectively protect themselves regardless of age, size or strength level. Noriyasu Kudo Sensei proves this on a consistent basis. He is a 75 year old master who can, and does, bang with the youngest most fierce martial artists, street fighters, and thugs the world has to offer (*with no problem*). How? I'll tell you how. His training has substance.

**Clarence Whitley Shihan
(Isshin Ryu) & Me (Seigyo Do Karate)**

10

CAN KARATE STOP A BULLET?

Many years ago, I was walking through a mall in Massachusetts with my friend Kevin. We ran into one of the most dedicated martial artists that I know, Kareem Sharif. I introduced Kevin to Kareem. We were having a great conversation up until Kevin asked this question, "Can karate stop a bullet?" Kareem instantly became pissed off, and advanced towards Kevin. What made matters worse, besides the fact that Kareem was born with a short fuse, was the fact that my intervention would be the only thing to save Kevin from serious bodily harm.

Can karate stop a bullet? The answer is, "yes". How? In order to answer that question we must first understand what karate actually is. Karate is not a sport, a business, or a hobby. It is a life-focusing activity. The average person imagines an Asian person in pajama-like clothing screaming, punching and kicking. Karate is constantly portrayed that way on the silver screen. True karate practice is nothing more than a vehicle leading the participant towards the ultimate goal of enlightenment.

True karate consists of punching, kicking, clinch work, grappling, joint manipulation, muscle disruption, vital point, and vital area attacks. If it has to do with fighting, the elite black belt does it. Hard training helps the practitioner understand the life lessons that are extracted from the physical. Those of us who try to follow some type of code of conduct have a better understanding about the subject at hand. Martial artist's interactions are different than the average person's. In fact, everything that a martial artist does, should stand out. Black belts should always be, "8 miles ahead, in a 5-mile race."

Everything that we do and say is a technique designed to set up our future. If it isn't a finish move or conversation ending statement, it is a control pointer leading to something bigger. Imagine this. I wake up in the morning on the wrong side of the bed and I'm less than cordial to the first person I see. Our interaction could have detrimental effects on everyone that that person encounters from that point on. Think about it. Because of my rude demeanor he/she are now in a worse mood than before he/she crossed my path. He/she could be in a terrible state of mind due to factors I had no idea existed. Maybe, a loved one passed, or that person just lost his/her job. Our interactions could be the straw that broke the camels back.

We never know how our interactions affect those around us. It would behoove everyone to treat all with respect. I work in what I would consider to be the most negative atmosphere in the world, a prison. I treat everyone with the utmost respect, regardless of his or her charge. You would not believe how my demeanor affects my interactions with the most violent, hardened criminals.

In the dojo we have mirrors adorning almost every wall. We are encouraged to gaze into those mirrors and look to develop the self. Not just the physical self, but every aspect of the self. Such as, self-control, the educated self, self-respect, etc . . . . So again, I ask you, "Can karate stop a bullet?" I would say, "yes." As **Michael Jackson** has stated several times, "It starts with the man in the mirror."

(S.M.A.R.T.) **S**pringfield **M**artial **A**rtists **R**ally for **T**ogetherness

11

THE ELITE

About seven years ago my ex-girlfriend and I were in a Massachusetts Sheriff's Department academy. Our academy class was run by one of the most intense martial artists of our time, Lt. Tommy Rondeau. He is, in my opinion, one of Noriyasu Kudo Sensei's best disciples. My ex holds a shodan ranking in Tae kwon do, and I hold rank in the art of karate.

Our academy class ran no less than seven miles a day. For people who don't normally run that's pretty intense, right!? Here's the thing. I hate to run. Running is definitely not one of my favorite pastimes, but if I have to do it, I will. As our group ran in formation, people would fall out along the roadside and begin to walk. My ex and I would run side by side, daily. One day, she was having a difficult time keeping up. She began to fall out to the side when I said to her, "There is no way in hell that you are going to fall out. We are black belts. The elite. You better suck it up." She kept running.

I know what you are thinking. You're thinking, "He thinks he's better than everyone else", or something along those lines. That couldn't be further from the truth. It's not that I think I'm better. I have to be better. You see, I lead people who look up to me everyday in my dojo. For that reason alone, I must model proper attitude. **I don't give up**. All, who wear dan (Black Belt) rank share the responsibility to be better.

Every aspect of our existence as a black belt has to be dedicated to creating a harmonious atmosphere for all to enjoy. We as dan holders share the responsibility of protecting the weak and educating the masses. The problem is that there aren't many qualified black belts out there. Most black belts in this day and age are self-promoted. Don't be discouraged. If you really observe someone's actions, you can tell who is a genuine black belt, and who isn't.

Tommy Rondeau Sensei & Me studying in-depth
Judo concepts

12

THE POSSIBILITY OF THE IMPOSSIBLE

While training in the martial arts, I've witnessed a lot of things I would've never believed could've been done. Kudo Sensei, Whitley Sensei and Okamura Sensei all have done some pretty unbelievable things to me, and around me. I have also heard stories of other instructors who have done some pretty amazing things. Some things that I will discuss will be hard to believe. All that I ask is that you keep an open mind as you read this.

Kudo Sensei is a man who has been a student of the martial arts for more than six decades. He has forgotten more information about the arts than I will ever learn in my lifetime. He and his Shito-Ryu instructor were in downtown Springfield, MA one night enjoying a night on the town when his Sensei decided to show him something. What came next is totally amazing. Kudo Sensei's instructor proceeded to kick a parking meter head off of its pole. How many people actually think they would ever see something like that in their lifetime? Kudo Sensei attempted the very same feat but he could only bend the pole. Which, is amazing to me as well.

Okamura Sensei's command of the Daito Ryu curriculum is unmatched. One day during a workout he proceeded to show me a fist position that was the key for unhinging a jaw. I thought, "How would someone have found that type of information out." Sensei approached me, grabbed the side of my face, and proceeded to demonstrate the technique. My jaw hasn't been the same since. Incredible, don't you think?

Whitley Sensei has not only burned me by nothing more than slightly touching me, but I have also seen him and his brothers takeout several people in the street like they were on a movie set. I've talked to martial artists who honestly believe those things are not possible. I'm here to tell you that it is most definitely possible.

Proper training, in the martial arts helps one to bust through that barrier that we are all burdened with at one time in our adulthood. The child's mother who lifts the car to save the child is one who realizes that there is no such thing as a barrier. It is nothing more than self-doubt. Masters of the martial arts have total control over their mind-state, and can command the energy needed to perform such tasks as mentioned above at "will".

W. Mark Whitley Shihan (Taikido Karate Kai Headmaster) &
Me

13

A VIVID IMAGINATION

In your opinion, what is the one ingredient that makes Stephen King one of the most accomplished writers of our time? Give up. It's his imagination. Most successful people are pretty imaginative. They usually think outside the box. Inventors, because of their ability to imagine their product, invent items that are useful.

Martial artists need to think that very same way during training, in order to be an effective student, fighter and teacher. In the art of Aiki Jujutsu as presented to me by my instructor, there are thirteen basic lessons. Each lesson has unlimited variations. The only thing that limits an individual is his/her own imagination. My imagination might only allow me to visualize two thousand variations of ikka-jo (first lesson/elbow locks). Your imagination might allow you to visualize five thousand variations of the very same technique.

I want you to use your imagination and see how many situations you can use a downward parry/block to address. Keeping in mind the principles of oyo and kakushi, should help you drastically. Every technique in your entire art should be evaluated this way. Also, it should have a high probability of working for everyone against anyone.

Our goal, in the self-protection aspect of the art is to reach a state of total awareness. Once one reaches the level where they're no longer restricted by a lack of imaginative ability, they will have transcended their skill to a more advanced state. At this point the individual is now eligible to wear the rank of **godan** (5th degree black belt).

I have discovered that we don't need an abundant amount of techniques. All we have to do is explore the limited techniques we do have. Each technique, no matter how simple, has a deeper inner working that can't be denied. With a little imagination and a "will" to explore, all things will present themselves. **Sherman Harrell Sensei** (Isshin Ryu) is the perfect example of one who has discovered an arts potential through deep research and dedicated practice. Train hard, be dedicated, and most of all imagine the possibilities.

The board of wisdom

14

IF YOU BELIEVE

If you take a moment to look back at situations that you have seen or experienced, I'm one thousand percent certain you will agree with the saying, "If you believe it to be true, it will be true." How many times have you heard stories about people that "will" themselves sick? That person goes to see a doctor who gives them some type of "dummy medication" to soothe their mind. All of a sudden, they get better!? Hmmmmm?

Within any activity, self-doubt is probably the most detrimental barrier that will disable a person. A long time ago, as a child, I constantly would tell people that I was good at gymnastics. Mainly, floor exercises. There were a couple of people in my neighborhood who fancied themselves as street gymnasts and I wanted to be known as one as well. Everything was fine, up until someone finally called me on it, and asked that I show and prove my claim.

I thought, "What the hell am I going to do now?" I did the only thing that I could do. I postured, on the lawn of the church across the street from my mother's house as if I was actually skilled in gymnastics. I hoped for some miracle to happen, that would allow me to escape. No such luck! As everyone waited, I made a resolve that I would try my hand and hoped for the best. I mean, what's the worst that could've happened? I watched gymnastics all the time. I should be able to imitate their movements.

Here goes nothing. I ran as if I were running the fastest 300 meter race that you've ever seen. I proceeded to execute a round-off. Immediately following the round-off, came a fairly smooth backhand spring that amazed everyone in attendance. Including me. I had done it. With no previous experience, I had completed a task that I apparently convinced myself that I could do.

I can't even tell you how relieved I was. I just hoped that no one would ask me to do it again. I am now, forty two years old. I can still to this day execute backhand springs, back somersaults, and a host of other gymnastics maneuvers like an old pro. My seventeen-year-old daughter enjoys when I perform them for her and her friends. I enjoy that I can as well.

The fact that I believed in myself helped me to achieve a skill that I always admired. I approach the martial arts the exact same way. I totally believe in my abilities. I know that I have a long way to go on this never-ending journey, and I'm going to enjoy cruising the scenic route. Hard training helps us to rid ourselves of self-defeating emotions, behaviors and thoughts, such as doubt. Do you believe?

Randy B. Haskins & Randi B. Haskins

15

CONFIDENCE = ENDURANCE

Michael Jordan is probably the most confident person who has ever played the game of basketball. Muhammad Ali was the most confident boxer to ever wear boxing gloves, and I have got to be the most confident aspiring martial artist/ martial scientist I know. What does it all mean? It means that we can go on forever in our chosen activity.

Michael Jordan is not the most skilled physically. We all remember that scene when Allen Iverson crossed-over on Jordan and almost broke his ankles. Iverson might have the superior ball handle over Michael, but Mike has the confidence to carry a team. Remember when Mike started playing for the Washington Wizards. The team as a whole began to play consistently better. His confidence carried over to the other players.

Remember the time Mike had a 102 temperature and still played the majority of the game. He outscored all those who were healthy on the court. Put Mike on a football field and I guarantee you he would get winded a lot easier. As Mike gained experience, his ability improved, which in turn, built his confidence.

Within the martial arts the older one gets, the better he/she gets. At least that's how it is supposed to work, but, in reality, fighters have been disproving that theory. I guess that's why we can't honestly call them martial artists. As one gets older and more experienced one should realize that, "*Skill is not determined by the physical, it is determined by what one comes to realize about the physical.*"

I've heard older body builders express that they regret the training they did when they were younger because they received injuries that could've been avoided. They were young, inexperienced, and overzealous. Now, in their advanced, they are confident in their ability to execute, as well as teach proper technique. They are also in the best shape of their lives. Confidence strikes again!

Can you drive a standard transmission vehicle? Do you recall how it was when you first attempted to hold on a hill at a light? How about when you were the first one in line at a red light, on flat land. Did you feel the pressure because of everyone waiting behind you. You probably stalled. Fast forward five years. I bet you drive while putting on lipstick, drinking coffee, talking on the cell phone, and chastising the kids, all at the same time. How did you get that way? Practice, that's how. Now your confidence is through the roof. No one knows your car the way you do.

The moral of this story is, with consistent practice one will gain valuable experience. Their skill will improve, and their confidence will be heightened to astronomical levels. An instructor's job is to act as a check and a balance. He/she must monitor the student's mentality, as to ensure the students confidence doesn't cross that fine line into the conceit realm.

My promotion to Hachidan 1/23/08

16

MARTIAL INSIGHTS

My thirty plus years of research have thus far consisted of, Aiki Jujutsu, Karate, Judo and Taiho Jutsu exploration. I have come to recognize an important point in the process. I have recognized that studying the "Martial Arts" is a limiting process. What we study within our organization (**UNDERGROUND ALLIANCE MARTIAL SCIENCE RESEARCH ASSOCIATION**) is the Martial Sciences.

The Martial Sciences are the understanding of; criminal law, physics, psychology, sociology, anatomy and martial arts (Technique) as it applies to combat. To further explain the difference between the two, a martial artist "can" punch and a martial scientist "understands how" to punch. UNDERSTAND THE DIFFERENCE?!?!

Regardless of the concept employed, (Sen no Sen/Go no Sen/Sen Sen no Sen). The principles behind the Martial Sciences tell us that we must ensure the "violence in our action" is never detected by our opponent. Through consistent, proper, practice, we will achieve an economy of motion unparalleled.

The physical act of training builds strong foundations, allows for freedom of expression, strengthens the spirit, conditions the mind, allows one to manage fear or uncertainty, and produces adaptability. Done properly, training will allow one to effortlessly perform any task.

I remember a conversation I had with an individual who witnessed the differences between his strike and mine. After this individual observed the affects of my strike, he stated, "You study a different style, that's why!" At which time, I informed him, "Effectiveness has nothing to do with styles, it has to do with information received, processed and explored."

There are many Martial Arts being perpetuated in the world today. MMA (Mixed Martial Arts) being the newest incarnation. Many speak badly about the "classical/traditional martial arts because of the many so called "masters" and their lack of knowledge, as well as their inability to successfully utilize the lessons learned in the dojo while on the streets.

All martial principles interconnect one way or another. With proper practice of kata, coupled with serious investigation of the history of the kata, anyone can unlock the mysteries surrounding true combat. As an intelligent individual, I recognize the "truth" that punching and kicking could not have been the only form of fighting back in the days when masters designed/developed their kata. Many, would have you believe different. Why wouldn't kata address other forms of combat?

Kata are unwritten textbooks that encompass complete fighting styles. Most study unrealistic bunkai (analysis) with no concept of the other three phases to exploring the information/lessons within the kata. The other phases are, (oyo, henka and kakushi). Remember, these arts were designed out of necessity, to address life-&-death combat! Karate is simply nothing more than a vehicle within the martial spectrum (when practiced correctly) designed to allow one to understand "Habitual Acts of Physical Violence." Techniques are nothing more than the individual tools used to physically "Fix" our problems. Don't "fight" people, address the situations at hand!

Rei (courtesies/etiquette) is an indispensable aspect of the learning process when it comes to the martial sciences. Those who don't employ it in their dojo/school/gym, hold students back from reaching their full potential.

As I sit here reflecting on teachings I've received from one of my instructors (Mark Whitley Shihan), I appreciate/ understand the lessons much more today than the day I received them. I was told, in a nutshell, "Don't be impressed with ones training, be impressed if the person/s can stand on the "line" and affect you!"

I've met many from here to Japan who were impressive in a room full of cooperative fighting partners. Well, **I DON'T COOPERATE** while fighting! In training we explore our weaknesses, fighting is where we exploit our strengths! We are supposed to develop the "Martial Arts" tools into sharp weapons of mass destruction by way of repetitious exploration propelled by unlimited understanding through researching, exploring and implementing the "Martial Sciences!"

As I mentioned in the beginning of this article, I established my own association and named it the "Underground Alliance Martial Science Research Association." We teach the **Seigyo Do** style of Karate. Seigyo defined is, "To keep superior situations against the attacking movements of the opponent in-order to control/beat the opponent."

I must take this time to clear up a misconception about exactly what Seigyo Do Karate is. Let me start by telling you what it isn't. Seigyo Do Karate is not a specific style. It is a theory that can be explored by any individual practicing any style or fighting form.

Seigyo Do Karate is made up of 68 core techniques divided up between 12 sections. Each technique has unlimited possibilities. The depth of each technique is limited by ones own imagination. Ones ability to devise smooth, flowing and effective combinations will come from their ability to read the situation at hand, and imagine the appropriate response.

I studied within the **KUDO KAI**, which is an association of martial artists who have come together under the leadership of Noriyasu Kudo Kancho. Kudo Kai member Mark Whitley taught me Karate. Kudo Kai member Takeshi Okamura taught me Aiki Jujutsu. Kudo Kai founder Noriyasu Kudo taught me Judo. Life experiences have taught me how to pragmatically use all I have learned.

The study of the martial sciences are most definitely a form of higher education. You must train with the mentality that you are fighting a trained attacker, and the understanding that the martial sciences were developed to defeat an untrained opponent. Let's face facts, anyone truly focused on training, life, career, family, education, etc . . . is not going to be out in the streets engaging in frivolous fights!

Students, Haniel Cotto, Juan Carlos Villanueva, Robert Turner and Jeremy C. Rivas meditating after class in the Underground Alliance Martial Science Research Association Hombu Dojo.

17

THE ART OF TEACHING

Individuals who approach and inquire about the martial arts have one of three mindsets: *The curious*, *the nonbeliever* or *the studious* mentality.

The curious is an individual who has interest in seeing what it is that a practitioner of the martial arts does but has no desire to experience it firsthand.

The non believer is an individual who would like to test the physical skill and fighting spirit of the instructor or other high-ranking officials of a martial arts organization.

The studious is an individual who has emptied his/her cup, and is ready to learn something different.

Once an individual's mentality is determined, and it is discovered that he/she is a possible candidate for acceptance as a student. It must now be determined which aspect of training should be focused on: *Body* (physical skill), *mind* (theory) or *spirit* (will to fight).

Organizations have their own individual ways of making believers out of non believers!

The purpose of this chapter is twofold. First, I'm going to educate you to a basic truth concerning rank. Secondly, I'm going to lay out a basic format for effective teaching. Within the realm of martial arts in the U.S., any, and everyone, who wears a black belt believes that they are a teacher (Sensei). The truth is, not everyone is blessed with the ability to teach. Receiving a black belt certificate of any degree does not qualify one to teach. In fact, that is only one of the criteria needed to achieve a teacher certification.

To teach effectively one must devise a lesson plan that will enable a student to visualize, experience, and live the material. Here is an easy-to-follow lesson plan, step by step.

Step 1: Choose a combination to be the focus of the session. Bow in.

Step 2: (15 min) Warm the body, utilizing safe exercises designed to build strength and muscular endurance.

Step 3: (15 min) After the body is warm, stretch and limber up using partner stretches. It is a lot harder to cheat yourself when you have a partner.

Step 4: Break down the combination into individual techniques, and work each technique on the forearm shields for 10 to 15 minutes apiece.

Step 5: Demonstrate the combination. Have the students work the combination on each other, without the focus pads or the forearm shields. Observe and correct mistakes. Remember, don't over correct them. This should happen for at least 15 minutes.

Step 6: Present other possibilities such as improper timing on tori's part, so the principle of henka can be explored.

Step 7: Discuss the theory behind the technique, and answer any questions the students may have.

Step 8: Bow out. Clean the dojo.

Note: Select warm-up exercises that would complement the body, as well as the combination. Change up the exercise routine so that the body doesn't begin to stagnate. You can adjust the time frame of each activity in order to lengthen or shorten the class accordingly.

18

MUTUAL BENEFIT

Approximately, sixteen years into my karate education my friend Phil (Tiger) came over to my house and informed me that there was someone who worked with him that he wanted me to meet. He wouldn't elaborate any further. I was curious, so I went to see who this mystery man was. We arrived at his workplace, and he immediately took me to the cafeteria, where the mystery would unfold.

As I walked into the cafeteria, I noticed a man who appeared to be of Asian decent. Phil Introduced me to the gentleman, who was sitting alone, totally absorbed in his food. "Casey, I would like you to meet Randy." I said, "Hi, nice to meet you." He sat there for at least five minutes, not saying a word, then all of a sudden he said, "Do you train?" I said, "yes." He then told me that it was nice to meet me. He didn't look up from his meal once, through the whole conversation.

About two weeks later Casey showed up at a training session that my karate instructor was leading. Whitley Sensei greeted him, had a short conversation, and then called me over. He instructed me to attempt to hit Casey. I wasn't sure what had just happened, but I followed the order. Sensei was irritated at my half-hearted attempt, and instructed me to do it again, only this time do it like I meant it.

As I advanced towards Casey, I sensed that something would be different this time around. Sure enough, Casey did something real swift and very painful to me. I was in a position that I did not recognize as being natural for any healthy young person. Casey held me in that position for a while as he continued to talk to Whitley Sensei. When I finally was released, I just stood there reflecting on the events that had just transpired.

I thought, "I have to learn from this man," but when I looked up he was gone. About one week later I was contacted, and told that Casey would be willing to take me on as a student. I was honored, as well as very excited. Casey turned out to be an instructor of Daito Ryu Aiki Jujutsu. Casey's birth name is Takeshi Okamura and he teaches his art at his house, in a private forum, to a small group of disciples.

When I was accepted as a student, he instructed me to select one person that I truly trust, and show them what was shown to me so that I consistently would have someone to work with. His logic was, we both would get something out of that arrangement. Each art has the principle of mutual benefit behind it, hence the terms uke (receiver of technique), and tori (giver of technique).

Uke practices his offensive techniques while tori practices his defensive techniques. They switch positions so they both get a feel for each other's position. Both individuals are now learning from one another. Anyone can hit something, but not too many people can receive technique. Neither one is more important than the other. It's all about balance. Mutual benefit.

Early on in my training I didn't understand that concept. I was constantly hurting my partners out of ignorance, and ego. All that is behind me now. All those around me will benefit from my training, you all have my word on that.

19

UNDERSTANDING THE CONNECTION

My entire life is dedicated to the research and development of life-effective martial arts. My motivation for life is my daughter, Randi B. Haskins. My karate is not something that I do, it is who I am. My life would be intolerable without Randi, or my training. Let's hope I never have to experience the loss of either.

My training has helped me to become focused in all other aspects of my life. I can only imagine where I might have been if I had not found my instructors. Not only has my focus improved. I also have a better understanding of the world as a whole. If one were to truly explore their chosen art, they would discover that many life lessons could be extracted from the physical act of hard training.

Due to the fact that Masutatsu (Mas) Oyama Sensei was constantly involved in negative activities, he was encouraged by his instructors to dedicate himself to his martial arts education. He became one of the world's most celebrated martial artists. He stated that his new focus in life was to, "Unify the world through the martial arts." He came pretty close to achieving his goal by establishing one of the largest, most successful organizations in the world.

While many other people in my neighborhood were selling drugs, committing predatory crimes, and "establishing their gangsta." I decided to dedicate myself to the research and practice of life-effective martial arts. I recall the day when someone I grew up with said to me, "There is more to life than karate." He, himself, lives for money. I am motivated by the desire to discover and develop a better me, and he lives for money. In his eyes, I'm the one who needs a new focus. Incredible, don't you think?

Gichin Funakoshi Sensei was a very sickly child, so his father enrolled him in a martial arts dojo. As a result of his training he developed into a strong young man. Martial arts strikes again! Another life improved by intense martial arts training. Funakoshi Sensei's body developed, which in turn strengthened his mind.

Here is a story that will help you to understand the point, that I have grown to understand as a result of my training in the martial arts. If you are religious, let me throw out this disclaimer right now: **By no means am I trying to offend anyone**!

Noah was just finishing up the loading of the ark when he spotted Jacob standing near the riverbank, staring off into the sky. Noah informed Jacob that he had room for one more, and would be willing to take him along. Jacob said, "No, my lord shall save me." The rain began to fall. Noah said, "Suit yourself." He closed the door to the ark, and sailed away. The water rose to the level of Jacob's chest, at which point a rowboat approached him. The occupants told him that they have room for one more, so he should seriously consider accepting a ride. Jacob informed them, "The most high shall save me." They shook their heads and rowed away. The water rose up to Jacob's nose. He was now standing on his tiptoes trying to breathe, to no avail. Jacob drowned. Walking toward the pearly gates, pissed off, he saw God and said to him, "What the hell happened? I waited for you!" God looked at him, took a deep breath, and said, "I sent you an ark, and a rowboat. What else did you want from me?"

The moral of that story is the same lesson I've come to learn through my martial arts training: "Adversity doesn't conquer individuals, lack of ambition does." What do you think?

20

WHICH ONE ARE YOU?

Do you really think "classical karate" and its kata have no true value when it comes to self-protection? If your answer is yes, this chapter might help you change your mind.

In sixteenth century Okinawa, individuals had to face threats that we, this day and age, could only imagine. The threat of death was very real. With that fact in mind, I ask, "Why wouldn't their training reflect that?" The laws were not as strict as they are today. Murder was a common activity back then. Common sense tells me that the practice of their art had to prepare them for real-world combat. Today, we face what I would call, "civilized threats."

With the threat of a civilized threat lurking around every corner, most training has become watered down and sports oriented. All of those so-called "reality fighters" are living in a fantasy world, believing that their training is the real-deal. When one faced the very real threat of being stabbed, decapitated, hung, tortured, maimed or killed one took his/her training very serious. One's training had to be able to address a variety of issues and circumstances because of the possible threats to ones survival.

Bruce Lee denounced classical kata, out of ignorance (lack of information). He did not have a clear understanding of the inner workings of the kata. I've had conversations with several people who wear high rank, and are ignorant of the true essence of their particular martial art. I'm sure the essay that I wrote entitled, "Transmission" has invoked some conversation as to the legitimacy of many systems active today. The scenario discussed in that article is very real. Situations like that have contributed to the lack of insight into the combat effectiveness of the classical martial arts.

So, how can we as instructors of the martial arts help the situation at hand? We must first, recognize that the threats that were faced many moons ago were very real. We must also understand, that martial arts truly addressed those issues. We now, have to be honest with ourselves, by recognizing that many forms of combat are addressed through the kata. Many forms and ranges of fighting, such as grappling, clinching, grabbing, striking and weapons. Lastly, long ago, kata itself was the main curriculum of all ryu. The lessons inherent in ones particular style were transmitted through the kata. Masters of yesteryear studied, and taught one, maybe two kata solely. Kata taught by the masters were very intense, and complete combat systems.

True exploration of one's art will reveal the deeper lessons inherent in the style. I have dedicated my life to the research and practice of life-effective martial arts. I treat all those who wear black belt rank as the elite, regardless if they can keep up or not. Those who can't keep up, embarrass themselves. Those who can, earn the respect of their peers. Which one are you?

From left to right: Clarence Whitley Shihan, Takeshi Okamura Shihan, Mark Whitley Shihan, Noriyasu Kudo Kancho, Chris Broughton Shihan, (Me) Randy B. Haskins, and Carey McKenzie Sensei.

21

INSIGHT 101

The lessons that I have learned through my martial science education can be summarized:

One is **FUELED** by their **HEART**, **GUIDED** by their **MIND**, and their actions are **PROPELLED** by their **DESIRE**. A true person of worth ensures that **HONOR DIRECTS** their every step, OSU!

Randy B. Haskins